Cello
Globetrotters

12 pieces in styles from around the world

Ros Stephen

MUSIC DEPARTMENT

OXFORD
UNIVERSITY PRESS

OXFORD
UNIVERSITY PRESS

Great Clarendon Street, Oxford OX2 6DP, England

Oxford University Press is a department of the University of Oxford.
It furthers the University's aim of excellence in research, scholarship,
and education by publishing worldwide

First published 2011
Reprinted with corrections 2014

ISBN 978-0-19-337004-3

Music and text origination by Julia Bovee
Printed in Great Britain on acid-free paper by
Halstan & Co. Ltd., Amersham, Bucks.

All the tunes in this book are original pieces by Ros Stephen.

Author acknowledgements: I am indebted to Juliet McCarthy for her invaluable help and advice.
I would also like to thank Philip Bagenal, Philip Croydon, Mary Chandler, Jane Francis,
Laura Jones, George McCarthy, Julian Rowlands, Sue Stephen, Keith Tempest, Daisy Vatalaro,
and all the wonderful musicians who played on the CD.

CD credits: Philip Bagenal (recording and mixing engineer), Gilad Atzmon (clarinet),
Javier Fioramonti (guitar), Pete Rosser (accordion), Daisy Vatalaro (cello), Yaron Stavi (double bass),
Jonathan Taylor (piano), Andy Tween (drums/percussion)

10. 'Hole in my Shoe' Blues

USA

Medium swing ♩ = 108

I've got a hole in my shoe,__ oh yeah! I've got a hole in my shoe,__ oh no!__ Well,

I've been walk-ing,__ walk-ing since the ear-ly morn-ing hours; now my sock is wet, what shall I do?__

I'm gon-na have to hop all the way to New Or-leans, oh poor me, I feel so blue.

A

I lost my mo-ney and my bus pass ex-pired. My bag is hea-vy and my legs are so tired.

Will I ev-er get there? Who knows? But if I do I will mend this shoe, that is for sure.

I'll get to New Or-leans some-how; some day I'll make it to your door.__

B

I've got a hole in my shoe,_ oh yeah! I've got a hole in my shoe,_ oh no!_ Well, I've been walk-ing,

walk-ing since the ear-ly morn-ing hours; now my sock is wet, what shall I do?_ I'm gon-na have to

molto rall. *trem.* + (LH pizz.)

hop all the way to New Or-leans, all I need is one new shoe, new shoe! Yeah!

Contents

Suitable for cello players of 3+ years' experience (grade 2 to 4 standard), the pieces are based on a wide variety of world music styles.

Each piece comes with background information about the musical style and warm-up exercises. As an additional resource, our dedicated website can be found at www.globetrotters-music.com

The accompanying CD includes authentic performance and play-along tracks for each piece, all recorded by a real band.

Cello accompaniment parts, suitable for a more advanced player or teacher, are provided for every piece, and piano accompaniments (with guitar chord symbols) for printing are included on the CD as PDFs. PC users can access the PDFs by selecting 'Computer' from the start-up menu and right-clicking on the CD drive to open the CD. Mac users should double-click on the data disc that appears when the CD is inserted to see the PDF files.

performance 1; backing 13

This tune is an Irish-style jig. Jigs are written in compound time, in this case 6/8, which means there are two dotted-crotchet beats (♩. ♩.) or two groups of three quavers (♪♪♪ ♪♪♪) per bar. Try saying 'one-and-a, two-and-a' to get the feel of the 6/8 rhythm. Watch out for the C♮s and F♮s in the second half of the piece and remember that they're played with the 2nd finger. Traditional Irish music tends to contain a lot of ornamentation. The ornaments are usually improvised so they can be different every time the tune is played. The ornament used in this tune is called a 'Cut', shown here as ⋎ (see Warm-up 1c, p. 28). The renowned Irish folk group 'De Dannan' featured a cello in many of their recordings.

cello accompaniment

5

2. Stoppin' off in Louisiana

Globetrotters

CAJUN, USA

Very rhythmic ♩ = 72

Easier version (melody only)

Very rhythmic ♩ = 72

This tune is in the style of a Cajun two-step. The Cajuns are French-speaking people who live in Louisiana in America. Although Cajun music is most commonly played on fiddle and accordion, early traditional American music was often accompanied by the cello, and several contemporary American folk groups, such as 'Crooked Still', feature the cello. Don't be put off by the double stopping—this isn't as hard as it looks. All you have to do is play an open string at the same time as the melody notes. Practise the warm-ups (p. 28) to get used to this, and also try playing the melody notes on their own, as in the 'Easier version'.

cello accompaniment

Medium bossa nova ♩ = 120

Bossa nova comes from Brazil in South America and is a slang expression that roughly translates as 'The New Thing'. It's a development of the samba, but has more complicated melodies and harmonies and is characteristically performed by guitar and voice. Although the music sounds relaxed it needs to be very rhythmic, so keep a solid tempo and pay attention to the syncopated rhythms; also watch out for the F♯s, G♯s, and C♮s. The warm-ups (p. 29) will help you with the rhythms and tuning.

Cello accompaniment

performance 4; backing 16

4. Dancing in Odessa

Klezmer is Jewish music from Eastern Europe and is characterized by expressive melodies, usually in minor keys, set against a strongly rhythmic accompaniment. Odessa is a town in Ukraine, famous for its Jewish cultural heritage. Traditional klezmer bands use instruments such as violin, clarinet, accordion, and double bass or tuba. 'Di Fidl-Kapelye' is an example of a klezmer band that includes cello, and the solo cello music of John Zorn, recorded by Erik Friedlander, is strongly influenced by Jewish music. This piece is a *freylekhs* (pronounced 'fray-lacks', a Yiddish word meaning joyful), which is a fast dance piece. It should be played very energetically with plenty of bow and strong accents.

Cello accompaniment

5. Shanghai Rickshaw Ride

Chinese bowed string instruments belong to the *huqin* family. The lowest-pitched of these is the *zhonghu*, which is played in a similar way to the cello but has only two strings. There is also a more modern instrument called the *gehu*, which combines the cello with the *zhonghu*: it has the same range as a cello but the body is a resonating box covered by snakeskin. Listen to the Hong Kong Chinese Orchestra to hear the instruments of the *huqin* family. Traditional Chinese music uses the pentatonic (five-note) scale; this piece uses D minor and D major pentatonics (see Warm-up 5a, p. 29).

cello accompaniment

6. Cairo Cradle Song

This tune is in the style of an Arabic lullaby, and should be played very gently and sweetly with some vibrato. The grace notes are played as acciaccaturas (see Warm-up 6b, p. 30). Watch out for the E♮s and B♮s when they occur after E♭s and B♭s, and make sure your E♭s and A♭s are nicely in tune in bar 7 and in the sixth bar of A (see Warm-up 6a). Cellos are often heard in Arabic orchestras, and the great Egyptian singer Umm Kulthūm performed with an ensemble that included a cello.

Cello accompaniment

Globetrotters
GREECE

Steadily and heavily ♩ = 104

This piece is based on a style of Greek folk music called *rebetico*. *Rebetico* songs are typically full of grief, passion, and romance, telling stories about the lives and misfortunes of ordinary people. In ancient Greece music played an important role in theatre and in military training. The traditional Greek instrument that is closest to the cello is the pear-shaped, three-stringed, bowed *lyre*. This tune should be played with plenty of bow and a full sound. Watch out for the change of key from G minor to G major.

cello accompaniment

Tango comes from Argentina in South America. San Telmo is a famous old district of Buenos Aires where you can see people dancing the tango at almost any time of the day or night. A *milonga* is a style of tango music and is also the term for a social tango dance. A traditional-style *milonga* is fast and lively, but this piece, influenced by the 'nuevo tango' music of Astor Piazzolla, is slow and, like much tango music, rather sad. It should be played expressively with vibrato and a sweet tone. The cellists José Bragato and Yo-Yo Ma have both recorded a lot of tango music.

cello accompaniment

Lively ♩. = c.72

This piece is based on a style of folk music called *chamamé* that comes from North Eastern Argentina. The Iguazu River is on the Argentinian—Brazilian border and has some of the biggest waterfalls in the world. Traditionally performed on accordion and guitar, *chamamé* is characteristically warm-hearted and upbeat music. In this piece the left hand of the piano is playing in 3/4 time while the melody is in 6/8 time; this is an example of polyrhythmic music (polyrhythmic means playing more than one rhythm at a time). See Warm-up 9a (p. 31) for help with these rhythms.

Cello accompaniment

10. 'Hole in my Shoe' Blues

Medium swing ♩ = 108

I've got a hole in my shoe,___ oh yeah! I've got a hole in my shoe,___ oh no!___ Well,

I've been walk-ing,___ walk-ing since the ear-ly morn-ing hours; now my sock is wet, what shall I do?___

I'm gon-na have to hop all the way to New Or - leans, oh poor me, I feel so blue.

A

I lost my mo-ney and my bus pass ex - pired. My bag is hea-vy and my legs are so tired.

Will I ev - er get there? Who knows? But if I do I will mend this shoe, that is for sure.

I'll get to New Or - leans some-how; some day I'll make it to your door.___

B

I've got a hole in my shoe,_ oh yeah! I've got a hole in my shoe,_ oh no!_ Well, I've been walk-ing,

walk-ing since the ear-ly morn-ing hours; now my sock is wet, what shall I do?_ I'm gon-na have to

molto rall.   trem.   + (LH pizz.)

hop all the way to New Or - leans, all I need is one new shoe, new shoe! Yeah!

The blues is a music of African—American origin dating back to the early twentieth century. It has had a strong influence on Western popular music, forming the roots of jazz, rhythm and blues, and rock. Blues songs are often sad, telling stories of hard lives, lost love, and misfortunes. This piece should be played with a 'swing' feel, namely quavers in a *long—short* pattern; see Warm-up 10a (p. 31). Listen to the recording (track 10) to hear how this is done, then try saying the words along with the recording. There have been several great jazz and blues cellists, such as Oscar Pettiford and Fred Katz.

cello accompaniment

performance 11; backing 23

11. Transylvanian Stick Dance

Heavily, with energy ♩ = 60

Transylvania is a region in central Romania renowned for its thrilling folk music, which inspired composers such as Bartók and Kodály. Transylvanian folk bands are traditionally made up of violin, three-string viola, double bass, cimbalom, and a percussive instrument called an *utogardon*. The *utogardon*, or 'beaten cello', is an ancient cello-shaped percussion instrument with four strings. The player hangs it around their neck and hits the strings with a stick, creating a strong rhythmic pulse. Imagine that you're playing an *utogardon* at letter A confidently; Warm-up 11a (p. 32) will help you with this. (but don't hit your cello!). The three-note chords should be played very

Cello accompaniment

Heavily, with energy ♩ = 60

This piece is based on the 12/8 'bell pattern' heard in the drumming music of the Ewe people of Southern Ghana (see Warm-up 12a, p. 32). The bell pattern is played on a special bell called a *gankogui* (or *agogo bell*) while a group of drummers, using a variety of different-sized drums such as the *sogo*, *kidi*, and *kroboto*, play several distinct 12/8 patterns simultaneously to create highly complex polyrhythmic music. The Ewe people also have a tonal drumming language known as 'talking drums' that can be used to communicate over long distances. Try singing or saying the words and clapping the rhythm along with the recording (track 12).

Cello accompaniment

1. Dublin Time

(a) BOWING PATTERNS

Try to make the slurs and string crossings smooth. Listen carefully to the tuning of the top C♮ in Exercise i and remember that it's played with the 2nd finger.

Ex. i

Ex. ii

(b) 2ND- AND 3RD-FINGER NOTES

This exercise will help you sort out the fingering for the F♯s and F♮s found in the second half of this piece.

(c) ORNAMENT: THE 'CUT'

To play this ornament, hold down the melody note (C) with your 2nd finger and 'cut' the string by flicking it with your 4th finger. It can also be played on 1st finger notes, again using the 4th finger to make the cut. The upper note should almost make a percussive sound rather than a melodic tone. See if you can find some other places in the piece to play this ornament.

↑ *'flick' 4th finger onto A string*

2. Stoppin' off in Louisiana

(a) DOUBLE STOPPING

Play this exercise slowly, listening very carefully to your tuning. Make sure your fingers don't touch the open-string notes.

make sure your fingers don't touch the open A   *get ready for the C♮*   *tune the octave Ds carefully*

(b) NOW A BIT QUICKER

Make sure that your bow is level over both strings and try to keep your left hand relaxed.

Ex. i   *Ex. ii*

(c) SLIDES

Cajun musicians often slide up to notes. Try sliding up to an F♯, as shown; slowly at first and then speeding up. When these feel easy, try sliding to the F♯s in bars 2, 4, and 6 of the piece. You could also try sliding up to the high Ds in bars 1, 3, and 5.

3. Relaxing in Rio

(a) BOSSA NOVA RHYTHM

Bossa nova tunes often contain syncopated rhythms. A syncopation happens when an accent falls on a weak, rather than a strong, beat. Clap these rhythms with your metronome set to ♩ = 120. The first rhythm is a commonly used two-bar bossa nova accompaniment pattern, and the second is the opening rhythm of the tune.

Rhythm i

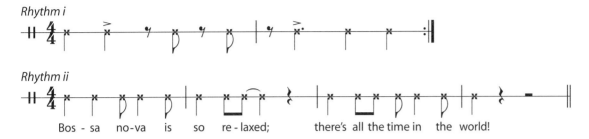

Rhythm ii

Bos - sa no-va is so re-laxed;   there's all the time in the world!

(b) INTONATION EXERCISE

Play this exercise slowly, listening carefully to the tuning of the 2nd- and 3rd-finger notes. This will help you get bar 7 and the seventh bar of B nicely in tune.

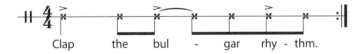

4. Dancing in Odessa

(a) *BULGAR* RHYTHM

The *bulgar* rhythm is a quick 3—3—2 rhythmic pattern often used in klezmer music. You'll play it three times in this piece; see if you can spot where. Try clapping the rhythm while saying the words.

Clap the bul - gar rhy - thm.

(b) BOWING PATTERNS

Some of the bowing patterns used in this piece are shown below. Practise these patterns on all the open strings until they feel comfortable. Use small, neat bows for the semiquavers (♪) and play the staccato quavers (♪) using two consecutive up-bow strokes, stopping the bow on the string between each stroke.

5. Shanghai Rickshaw Ride

(a) PENTATONIC SCALES

Try playing the two pentatonic scales used in this piece. The first is D minor and the second is D major.

D minor pentatonic scale

D major pentatonic scale

29

(b) ACTIVITY IDEAS

- The black notes on a piano form a pentatonic scale. Try making up a tune on the piano just using these notes; it's easy, even if you don't play the piano. Hold down the sustaining pedal and listen to the sound.
- Try making up your own pentatonic melody on your cello using the notes of one of the scales in 5(a).

6. Cairo Cradle Song

(a) HALF-POSITION NOTES

Half position is when your left hand moves back a semitone from first position. In the first exercise make sure you move far enough back to get the 1st finger E♭ nicely in tune, and stay in half position for the 2nd finger A. You'll do this in bar 7. When this feels confident, try sliding from the 3rd finger F♯ down to the 1st finger E♭. You'll do this in bar 6.

(b) ORNAMENTS

The ornaments in this piece are played as acciaccaturas. Literally meaning 'crushed notes', these should be played on the beat as quickly as possible. Play them slowly first, then speed them up. Lift the 2nd finger off cleanly and quickly. See if you can find other places in the piece to play an acciaccatura.

↑ quick 'crushed' note,
played on the beat

7. Acropolis Dance

(a) G HARMONIC MINOR SCALE

Listen carefully to the tuning of the interval E♭–F♯ (an augmented 2nd) in this scale.

(b) INTONATION EXERCISE

Play bars 16 and 18 (written out below) slowly. In bar 16 make sure that you extend back far enough with your 1st finger for the B♭, and take care with the tuning of the 1st finger E♭ and 1st finger A♮ in bar 18.

Bar 16 (4 before 'B')   Bar 18 (2 before 'B')

30

8. Tango in San Telmo

(a) TANGO PERCUSSION

Tango musicians often use their instruments to make percussive sounds. Techniques include *chicharra* (Spanish for cicada), in which the bow plays behind the bridge on the binding of the D or G string to make a scratchy sound, and *tambor*, in which the body of the instrument is tapped with the left hand. Try playing some of these percussive sounds using the rhythms shown below; you could play these during the four-bar introduction.

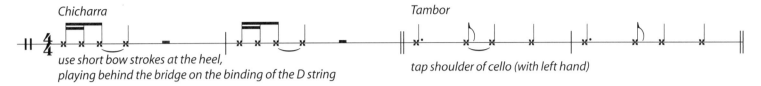

Chicharra

use short bow strokes at the heel,
playing behind the bridge on the binding of the D string

Tambor

tap shoulder of cello (with left hand)

9. Iguazu Rapids

(a) RHYTHM EXERCISES

Chamamé melodies often move between two- and three-beat rhythmic patterns, and a two-against-three rhythm is often heard in the accompaniment. Clap the rhythmic patterns below along with your metronome.

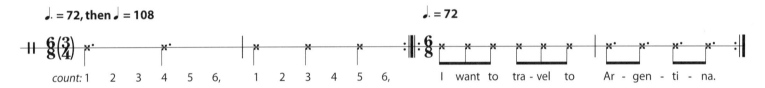

♩. = 72, then ♩ = 108

♩. = 72

count: 1 2 3 4 5 6,   1 2 3 4 5 6,

I want to tra-vel to Ar-gen-ti-na.

(b) BOWING EXERCISES

Play in the middle of the bow using small, neat strokes for the semiquavers (♪). Try the first exercise on all the open strings.

Ex. i   *Ex. ii*

Now try playing a D major scale using the rhythm and bowing pattern shown in Ex. i, changing note on the half bar.

Argentina
USA

10. 'Hole in my Shoe' Blues

(a) SWING RHYTHM

In these exercises the swing quavers (♪) are written out as triplets, which is the closest way of notating their *long—short* rhythm. They aren't written like this in the piece because it would make the music hard to read, so you have to remember to play all the quavers with this rhythm. Be careful not to hurry; it should sound relaxed and laid-back. Try these on all the open strings.

Ex. i   *Ex. ii*

I've got__ a hole in my shoe,__ oh yeah!   Walk-ing since the ear-ly morn-ing.

(b) ACTIVITY IDEA

Blues music, like jazz, often contains improvisation. This means that you make up your own tune on the spur of the moment. Start off by playing the C blues scale shown below. Next, think of a simple four-bar question-and-answer phrase like 'Who can play a blues tune on their cello? I can play a blues tune on my cello'. Pick a note from the scale and try playing the rhythm of your phrase; when this feels easy, pick a different note. Then try using more than one note, or try a slightly different rhythm. Now you're improvising! Mix the notes up; they sound great in any order. When this feels confident, try improvising along to CD track 25.

C blues scale (swing)

11. Transylvanian Stick Dance

(a) THREE-NOTE CHORDS

The three-note chords in this piece should be played quite heavily. Make sure that your bow is resting on both the G and the D strings before you start the chord. Play the two open strings together strongly, then quickly pivot your bow over to the A string to play the B, allowing the open strings to ring. Start this exercise slowly and gradually speed it up.

(b) ASCENDING MELODIC MINOR SCALE

This piece uses the notes of an ascending D melodic minor scale, as shown below. This scale is often heard in Romanian folk music and was used by the famous composer Béla Bartók.

Try playing it using the rhythm and bowing from letter A:

12. African Jamboree

(a) 12/8 RHYTHMIC PATTERNS

Try counting, clapping, and saying the rhythms shown below before you play the piece. The first rhythm is the West African 'bell pattern' and the second is the rhythm of the opening melody.

West African bell pattern   *Opening melody rhythm*

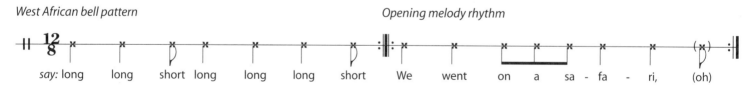

(b) BOWING PATTERNS

This open-string exercise will help you get the hang of some of the string crossings and bowing patterns used in this piece.